STRESS-BUSTERS FOR HOUSEWIVES

Kill The Silent Killer

Seema Gupta

V&S PUBLISHERS

Published by:

V&S PUBLISHERS

F-2/16, Ansari road, Daryaganj, New Delhi-110002
☎ 23240026, 23240027 • *Fax:* 011-23240028
Email: info@vspublishers.com • *Website:* www.vspublishers.com

Regional Office : Hyderabad
5-1-707/1, Brij Bhawan (Beside Central Bank of India Lane)
Bank Street, Koti, Hyderabad - 500 095
☎ 040-24737290
E-mail: vspublishershyd@gmail.com

Branch Office : Mumbai
Jaywant Industrial Estate, 1st Floor–108, Tardeo Road
Opposite Sobo Central Mall, Mumbai – 400 034
☎ 022-23510736
E-mail: vspublishersmum@gmail.com

Follow us on: t f in

© **Copyright:** *V&S PUBLISHERS*
Edition 2018

Printed at Repro Knowledgecast Limited, Thane

Dedicated to.....

All those housewives
who love to live
a stress free life

Acknowledgements

I would like to take this opportunity to thank a few people who helped me make this dream a reality.

First of all, I must thank my mother-in-law, Mrs. Avdhesh Gupta who taught me the intricacies of life and value of relationships.

Besides the all round help and unfailing support extended to me by my husband, Mr. A.K. Gupta and my daughters, Aashima and Ameesha. I wish to acknowledge my sincere thanks to Mr. Ram Avtar Gupta, Managing Director of Pustak Mahal for his support and encouragement to me to author this book. Without his support and encouragement, this book would not have been possible.

I also extend my grateful thanks to Mr. S.K. Roy, Executive Editor of Pustak Mahal for his unfailing help and guidance. It is his faith in my abilities which enabled this book to see the light of the day.

—**Seema Gupta**

Contents

Stress – The Silent Killer

'To me, the very essence of education is the concentration of mind and not the collection of facts.'

— Swami Vivekananda

'The real difficulty is always in ourselves, not in our surroundings.'

— Sri Aurobindo

During *Surya Namaskar*, each morning, when the bright sun rays touch my face gently, I feel light and relaxed. As the day progresses, the weight of emotions bogs me down and I wish for another ray of light from divinity to give me a fresh lease of life.

For a long time, I kept introspecting as to what makes us tense and unhappy. I ended up relating each day with the four phases of life. The early morning hours, when we are at our happiest and most relaxed, are like the carefree days of our childhood. As the day progresses, work mounts, expectations increase and there is a pressure to prove oneself – stress begins its journey through adolescence. By the time, our day progresses towards the post noon period, we are huffing and puffing to achieve our targets with tension mounting each second, quite like adulthood in life when we are working continuously without realizing how stressed out we are. Finally, it is time to close the shop. We are tired, stressed and devoid of energy. Our body and mind are craving for a break. So we call it a day – yes, the old age is creeping in.

But there have been times when we all feel very happy throughout the day. This clearly indicates that we have the power to conquer stress bodily, emotionally, intellectually and spiritually.

The first thing that comes to our mind is how do we define **STRESS**! Is stress a frown on our forehead or shaking of our hands in anger?

Stress is not something that affects us from outside. It is not an acquired trait by some unfortunate individuals. Stress is an integral part of the physical and mental system in all of us. We have inherited it during the course of evolution as a vital ingredient for normal functioning of the body. **Stress can be defined as a form of tension in our body or mind for which there is no release.**

Stress helps us in our survival on a sustained basis. But unchecked and uncontrolled stress can cause more harm to us than help. It can act as a **silent killer** and can erode our immune system leaving us vulnerable to many physical, psychological and personality disorders.

In simple words, stress is something that happens to our body whenever we are faced with a challenging situation.

The world witnessed stress for the first time when life itself originated on earth. Remember, the Darwin's theory of **'Survival of the Fittest'**. For people in those times also, it would have been equally stressful having to fight for each morsel, an inch of space or merely trying to survive. Stress always was and still is vital for our survival.

Does that mean stress is not bad for us? Exactly, that's the point!... In fact, stress is a motivating factor in our lives. However, the continuous and accumulating stress is detrimental to our mental and physical well being. We need to tame our feelings. Its optimum level provides the best opportunities to surging talents, energies and happiness.

We need not make any effort to get rid of stress because it would be futile. What we need to understand is that stress should be positive and conducive to our survival.

Stress in Joint Families

One day Akbar asked Birbal, "Tell me the difference between truth and falsehood in two words. Birbal said, "Four fingers." "Four fingers?" asked the Emperor, perplexed. "Your Majesty, what you see with your own eyes is the truth, but what you heard may not be true. The distance between one's eyes and one's ears is about four fingers, Your Majesty." said Birbal, grinning.

You see in others only what is in yourself.

You can't see faults in others unless the same faults exist in your.

The world is a laboratory where we conduct various types of experiments to learn various things and we ourselves are also tested off and on by facing various trials.

Unless you are ready to accept responsibility for the condition in which you are, there is very little that can be done to change that condition.

The best way to keep yourself happy is to ensure that others are happy.

Pressure Gauge

When you understand, you don't judge

Every young girl dreams of a family where she is treated like a princess. She enters matrimony laced with rosy dreams. But real life is a far cry from her dreams. When reality hits her hard, all her dreams come crashing down.

Stress Factor

When Sejal married, she had stars in her eyes. After the initial days of merry making were over, slowly the responsibilities started suffocating Sejal. She constantly complained to her husband that he never takes her out and doesn't bring her gifts often. They lived in a joint family so their house was always flooded with relatives. This would put an extra burden on Sejal. Sejal hated every moment doing house hold chores. But expectations from her in-laws made her slog the whole day long. She would crib and carry on with her work with a sullen face.

Stress Buster

Life is ever changing. Remember the time you were young. The way everyone cuddled you and coochie-cooed you then, is not done once you grow up. You assume different dimensions in various relationships and they keep on changing with time. There was a time when your mother would feed you, but as you grow up, you start feeding yourself. You accepted this as a part of your life. Similarly, you should accept the fact that you are now married and have to fulfil the responsibilities which come with it.

Say No to Stress

If the pressure in too much, it would be better to confide in someone who can make your in-laws understand your predicament. That person can be your sister-in-law, brother-in-law or your husband. Do not feel stressed as this is also a passing phase and you will soon get over it.

Creative Thinking

Enjoy the golden days of your life. Smile and everyone will smile with you. Soon, you will find many hands to help you and share your burden.

TIP OF THE DAY

When you feel stressed and want to shout, then go out to a lonely spot and yell and scream and stamp your feet. It does you good as well as to others - it stops you from thumping someone else.

Dowry – A Burning Issue

There is always a power within you
which is greater than all the odds
which can ever come to you in your life

There was a time in India when dowry was a burning issue and many young brides became its victim. With the intervention of the Government and NGOs, new laws were passed and the Anti Dowry Bill was passed by the Parliament. Even after so many corrective measures, the fear of dowry still looms large in the mind of our brides which makes them feel insecure.

Stress Factor

This reminds me of a funny incident which happened in our neighbourhood. When my neighbour, Mr. Khanna's only son got married, the bride came accompanied with all the dowry, as was asked by the Khannas. Except for demanding a few special items as dowry (as is the custom in their community), the Khannas, were basically nice people. But how was the new bride to judge this in a matter of a few days? After the couple came back from their honeymoon, the bride observed a bottle of kerosene oil kept in the kitchen with special care. On her own, the new bride decided that this bottle was kept there to burn her if she refused to bring any more dowry for them. One fine day, the television set she had brought as part of the dowry, broke down. The mother in-law was quite upset. Now the bride was very scared. She thought that she will be asked to replace it, which they did but only because all the papers were with the bride's father and the set was under guarantee. Unable to understand their view point, she refused to talk to her parents about the TV set at all and went into her room. As luck would have it, the electricity went off around one o' clock that night. This girl woke up when she heard some low voices coming from the kitchen. She could hear someone talking about kerosene and match box. Immediately, she came to the conclusion that her in-laws are planning to kill her by setting her on fire. She was under so much stress, that she could not think straight

and instead of acting rationally, she just raised an alarm over nothing. The whole neighbourhood collected only to discover that the Khannas were actually trying to light a kerosene lamp. They were doing so in a hush hush manner so as not to disturb the young couple. Just imagine, what an embarrassing situation was created due to stress over an imaginary problem!

Creative Thinking

Does this give you an insight! However, if you feel that you are genuinely facing a threat, then do not delay things.

Take someone in confidence and take corrective measures immediately. Because it's your life.

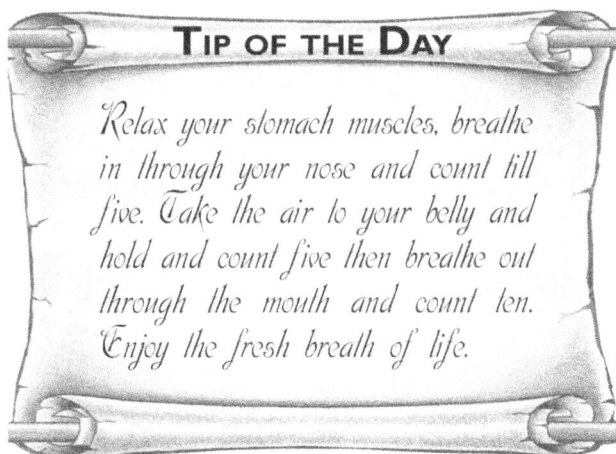

TIP OF THE DAY

Relax your stomach muscles, breathe in through your nose and count till five. Take the air to your belly and hold and count five then breathe out through the mouth and count ten. Enjoy the fresh breath of life.

Daughter vs Daughter-in-law

Look deep inside,
things are seldom what they seem.

This is a very sensitive issue. A girl who spends twenty years of her life with her biological parents, is suddenly sent to a new house to spend the rest of her life amidst total strangers. However, much she may try, she cannot become the daughter of the house overnight.

Stress Factor

Shweta and her husband's sister Mala were almost of the same age. When Shweta got married, Mala was in her final year in college. Initially, the two of them became good friends. But as time passed, Shweta could distinctly feel the discrimination made by her in-laws between herself and her sister-in-law. Mala was allowed to wear all kinds of clothes, she could boogy with her friends, she could get up late, she need not cook proper meals in the kitchen and she was never ever spoken harshly by anyone. The treatment meted out to Shweta was totally in contrast. Shweta missed her parental home where she was he cynosure of all eyes. Shweta felt suffocated and her behaviour towards her new family started showing signs of rebel.

Stress Buster

You have entered a new house where people are new, the rules are new. It takes time to adjust in a new place. Remember, you spent twenty years in that house which you considered your own. Now, how can you expect this house to become your own in just a matter of few days or weeks? Your sister-in-law has been here since birth, naturally, she feels the same as you feel towards your parental home. She is obviously getting the similar treatment which you were getting in your home before marriage. So have patience. Do not be hasty in making any decision. Each passing day will bring you closer to your new family.

Say No to Stress

As you become familiar with your new family, they too will begin to respond to you. No point in getting agitated over trivial matters and comparing yourself with your sister-in-law. Instead of competing, give her love and affection and rest assured, you will be reciprocated with similar feelings.

Creative Thinking

You may not be their daughter, but you are their daughter-in-law whom they have chosen with care, love and affection.

Why would they demean you? Put all the prejudices aside and love them like your own parents if you want to be their daughter. Soon, you will be more dearer to them than their own daughter.

TIP OF THE DAY

Be a dreamer. Allow yourself a dream time. Imagine yourself being carried away to a dreamland in your imagination. Return to this world refreshed and renewed. Remember, if you don't have dreams, they cannot come true.

Envy

> Happiness is a positive cash flow

1 n a joint family, it is a common notion that wives of two brothers are always at loggerheads. Initially, they may live in harmony but as children arrive and the monotony of daily routine takes over, envy and tensions become the way of life.

Stress Factor

Ruby and Sheena were good friends. They were married to two brothers. They lived in a joint family. Ruby was married to the elder brother. When Sheena came to the house as Ruby's younger sister-in-law, Ruby was ecstatic. Sheena also reciprocated her feelings. But as days passed by, various other emotions took over and the congeniality was replaced by envy and bickering between the two sisters-in-law. There was tension between them all the time. Fights among their children only added fuel to fire. Life became hell in that house with tempers rising at the slightest pretext.

Stress Busters

The elder sister-in-law has spent more time with the family than the younger sister-in-law so it is her duty to introduce the younger one to the new house. The younger sister-in- law, on the other hand, should give due respect to the elder one, as she is elder to her in age as well as in status. A little understanding and tact can go a long way. Fighting over children and their skirmishes is a foolish thing to do. Children forget and forgive more easily than elders. If you interfere in their matters, then you will only spoil your own relationships.

Say No to Stress

Who would like to live in a stressful environment? This will not only affect you but your children and other members of the family as well. Why should you envy each other? By living under the same roof, life can be very comfortable and enjoyable, but only if you maintain good relations.

Creative Thinking

United we stand, divided we fall

Always remember this adage. Be there for each other in times of need. Instead of envy, spread love and trust and see your relationship blossom.

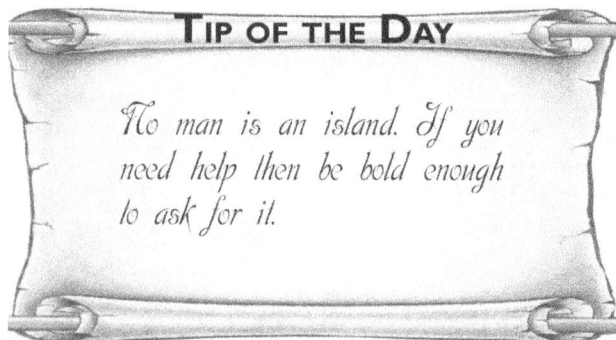

TIP OF THE DAY

No man is an island. If you need help then be bold enough to ask for it.

Interfering Relatives

> Nobody is happy all the time,
> but that is no excuse for being miserable.

Life in a joint family is not a bed of roses if there are interfering relatives who dominate the thought process of the master or the lady of the house. If you are a working woman then you can escape these episodes by being away from home for better part of the day, but if you are a housewife, you have to bear the brunt stiffly.

Stress Factor

Raju and Meeta were married for two months. Meeta's mother-in-law Sharada, gave them lot of time together and did most of the work herself.

Life was peaceful until the day, Sharada's sister, Vimla came from Ahmedabad to spend a few days with the family. She was a very dominating person. She did not like the way her sister was handling her daughter-in-law. She influenced Sharada to bring the young bride to task and put all the household chores on her shoulders. Sharada relented and all hell broke loose for Meeta. She kept praying for the lady to leave.

Stress Buster

Putting up a war in such situations will not take you anywhere. 'Endurance' is the keyword. Wait for a few days. Let the high tide pass. As the tempers cool down, you will find it easier to get your point across.

If the relative is a guest in your house for a few days, then bear things with patience because soon it will be time for her to leave. Then you can go back to your normal routine. But if the person interfering is a member of your family then you need to talk things out as early as possible.

Say No to Stress

Do not feel so stressed. There is no problem in this world which has no solution. You can win anyone with love, affection and endurance. Getting stressed only makes matters worse.

Since you are a housewife, you will be interacting with them all day long. So instead of putting up a war front and facing them as your worst enemy, why not mingle with them and win their hearts? It may be tough, but not impossible.

Creative Thinking

An old saying goes —

If you can't win them, join them.

This will be much better than living with the stress of having them as your critics forever.

TIP OF THE DAY

There is a Rose flower remedy for nearly every emotion. If you do not want to find out about all your emotions, then taking their rescue remedy will give you relief from many common emotional upsets. So discover the comfort in the essence of the Rose - calm is just a few drops away.

Stress in Nuclear Family

Emperor Akbar once asked Birbal, "Birbal is there anything that the sun and the moon cannot see?"

"Yes, Your Majesty, Darkness," came the prompt reply from Birbal.

In dwelling, live close to the ground,
In thinking, keep to the simple,
In conflict, be fair and generous,
In governing, don't try to control,
In work, do what you enjoy,
In family life, be completely present.

If you can take care of things,
which are in your hands,
things which are not in your hands,
will be automatically taken care of.

No one was ever really taught by another.
Each one of us has to teach oneself in the long run.

Living Alone

> When men and women are able to respect
> and accept their differences, then love
> has a chance to blossom

Living in a nuclear family is very different from living in a joint family. The concept of the nuclear family came into existence when India became global. The rural population started moving towards cities in search of better career prospects. Naturally, it was not possible for the whole family to move to a new place and abandon their roots altogether. So the immediate family such as the husband, wife and kids migrated. This new found freedom from the clutches of old family traditions gave them new wings and soon, the nuclear family became a big concept. Their stressors may be different from a joint family set up, but stress in a nuclear family cannot be totally ruled out.

Stress Factor

Sheela migrated to Delhi from Jaipur, when her husband got a new job. She was very happy at having escaped the domineering mother-in-law and the never ending house hold chores in her in-laws' house. When her husband went to office, she would finish all the chores quickly and relax. Sometimes, she would go for shopping. She felt relaxed and very happy. But the initial euphoria soon died and she started feeling very lonely in the house. She was used to living in a house full of people with their continuous chatter filling up every moment of the day. Here she hardly had anyone to talk to. There were no friendly neighbours and her hubby would be away for most part of the day. In the evening, he would be so tired that they hardly went out, except for the weekends. She felt that she lived only on weekends. Rest of the week stretched before her like a hot sandy road which she dreaded to tread. She started feeling tense as Monday approached.

Stress Buster

Living alone can be very taxing emotionally. You may enjoy the initial freedom but later on, when you are left in an empty house the whole day long, you may start dreading the long and lonely hours, especially, if you do not have a very friendly neighbourhood.

So the better way to deal with the situation is by making friends or keeping yourself occupied in various activities of your choice. You may join a hobby course which would not only enhance your skills but will also keep you occupied and give you an opportunity to meet people and make friends other than your neighbours.

Say No to Stress

The stress of having to while away the hours shows in your interaction with your husband when he comes back from work. You become more demanding. You need to go out more often because human beings are social beings and we need to interact with people. So come out of your shell. Big cities may sound aloof, but they also open many avenues for people and give them a chance to take part in group activities.

Creative Thinking

Remember, how you loathed the never ending housework in the joint family and how you treasure your privacy and independence here. Every situation has its own virtues and vices. So count your blessings and learn to adjust in every situation.

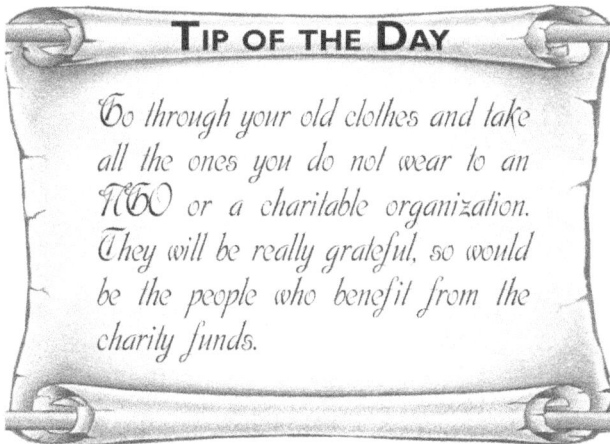

TIP OF THE DAY

Go through your old clothes and take all the ones you do not wear to an NGO or a charitable organization. They will be really grateful, so would be the people who benefit from the charity funds.

Resourceful

> No worry is bigger than your peace of mind

I n a joint family, you pool in your resources and run the household. In this way, the burden does not fall on a single person's shoulders. But in a nuclear family, the entire responsibility of running the household falls on the only earning member of the family, since the housewife is not earning so her contribution in monetary terms is negligible.

Stress Factor

Ritu's husband was an accounts officer in a private firm. But as the family grew and the cost of living went up, his income became insufficient in meeting the expenses. He picked up a part-time job. Life became very monotonous for Ritu as her husband became irritable with so much of work pressure. He would come home late and would be always tired. There was always shortage of money in the house and she had to be careful with the expenditure. Ritu was fond of going out and having fun but no luxuries were permitted in their existing budget. Ritu started feeling suffocated in this kind of atmosphere at home.

Stress Buster

In today's times, this situation may rise in any household. With constant rise in inflation, naturally, the husband has to work harder to make both ends meet. He may feel overworked and take out his stress on you. This gives rise to conflicts and the marital harmony may get disturbed. In such a situation, you are left with two options,either approach his parents or your parents and seek financial help or cut down on your expenses. If he is working so hard to maintain a dignified profile then why can't you sacrifice some material comforts for him and share his burden?

Say No to Stress

Your husband may be tired because of working overtime and coming late from office. This is a stressful situation for a housewife who spends the entire day waiting for her husband. In return, she does not get even a loving smile from her tired husband on his return. Secondly, spending lavishly on luxury items would become difficult because you need to save for the rainy days too. All these factors together make a very stressful condition. But do not feel disheartened. Times do not always remain the same. On your part, you can also make an effort and try to organize something from home which can bring you financial relief — like taking up a part time job or saving money on little things and by not being extravagant.

Creative Thinking

Stress is a part of our lives but letting it consume our lives completely will be pathetic. So find your happiness in small measures of everyday life and keep your cool. Remember if there is a problem, there has to be a solution nearby.

TIP OF THE DAY

Stimulate and nourish your mind by eating food for thought.

Choline in vegetables and eggs aid memory.

Inositol in grapefruit and cabbage nourishes brain cells.

Carbohydrates in pulses, rice and potatoes provide essential energy for our brain.

Mood Swings

> Listen to your own voice,
> when you ignore it, you suffer the most

Your husband's mood swings can be easily controlled by a light scolding by his family members who are more prominent in a joint family. Since you are the only one around the house in a nuclear family, most of the time you become a victim of his wrath.

Stress Factor

Ruchika's husband was very particular about keeping things in place whereas Ruchika herself was not such a perfectionist. She liked to keep things clean and tidy but not to the point when you cannot even relax on the sofa or enjoy a meal without having to worry about spilling the curry on the mat. But her husband was tidy to the tiniest detail. As evening approached, Ruchika would become a wreck as she did not know what might irk him and spoil the mood. The children would be huddled in their own room as their father's arrival came nearer. The same Ruchika who was a jolly and warm person when she lived in a joint family turned cold and withdrawn now. She felt helpless, not knowing whom to turn to for her husband's mood swings.

Stress Buster

If the husband is a perfectionist, then it becomes a routine which can be very stressful to you. You may take your husband to be a heartless person who does not seem to care a bit for your feelings. Try to understand his predicament also.

He has lived so many years of his life with his perfection, so you cannot expect him to change overnight.

You can either make him see your point of view tactfully or take help of an elder person who has influence on him. The routine shoving of children in their room for the fear of spoiling the cushions or the seating arrangement is not good for their psyche. So take measure before it is too late.

Say No to Stress

Don't look at your husband reproachfully. Everyone has his faults. If you were in his place, your mood swings would equally be stressful to the husband and kids because when they try to find respite in the cool confines of a home, you would pounce on them for no fault of theirs.

Such situations arise only in nuclear families because there is no set code of conduct as is mostly found in joint families.

Creative Thinking

Before you get stressed, just imagine the kind of stress he must be facing on returning from office and while standing in front of the door. Being a perfectionist, his worst fears would be not to find things in place. Sympathize with him and do not be angry with him. Help him to get over his phobia.

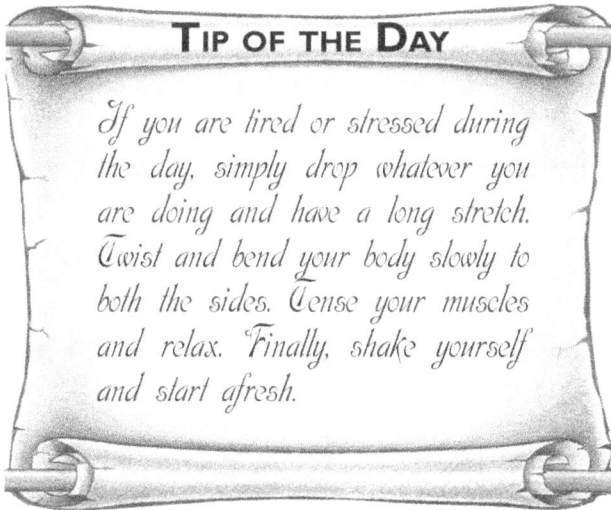

TIP OF THE DAY

If you are tired or stressed during the day, simply drop whatever you are doing and have a long stretch. Twist and bend your body slowly to both the sides. Tense your muscles and relax. Finally, shake yourself and start afresh.

Rejection

> I suggest that it is your judgements which keep you from joy and your expectations which make you unhappy

When you marry in a family, you want to become a part of that family. It takes efforts on both side to develop a compatible relationship. In most of the houses, if the daughter-in-law lives separately then she is rejected and considered as an outsider while the son remains to be a member of that family.

Stress Factor

Shruti lived with her in-laws but she was constantly ridiculed for bringing insufficient dowry. She was trying her best to adjust with them when suddenly, her husband got transferred to a different city. It was a God sent solution for Shruti through which she could escape this stressful situation without much melodrama. They managed to set a separate home in the other city. But what irked Shruti most was the fact that her in-laws started treating her as an outsider. She was neither consulted in any family matter, nor was she apprised of any family functions, whereas her husband was posted of all the details. Shruti felt dejected and depressed. For no fault of hers, she was labelled an outsider.

Stress Buster

The in-laws may not take kindly to a daughter-in-law who lives separately. This is an underlying stress because you lose a coveted position in the family. You may feel like an outsider when you are neither consulted nor told about the major decisions taken in the family. It is the time for you to take some steps. You can make some more efforts and improve your relations with the family members. It would be easier now, since you are living away from them and have already created your own space. Your efforts will not go unnoticed and sooner or later, either they will accept you or your husband will force them to accept you.

Say No to Stress

Your husband would never face such a problem because he is never blamed for the separation. It is always the daughter-in-law, who is not able to adjust and is thought to have taken the husband away from the cosy confines of his parental home. This unnecessary blame may make you tense. But say no to stress. Make efforts to carve your own place in this house.

Creative Thinking

If you wish to enjoy your freedom, do so in a subtle manner without hurting anyone. This will keep you stressfree and give you real happiness.

TIP OF THE DAY

If you are feeling very tensed, a cold shower leaves you feeling warm, invigorating and awake.

My Hands are Full

> We cannot direct the wind,
> but we can adjust our sails.

Bringing up small children is a big job. In a joint family, you get help from experienced people like your mother-in-law or your sister-in-law. But in a nuclear family, you may find yourself alone, nervous and fearful. Being inexperienced, you fear every move because you are not sure what is good for the baby. So you may either be running to the doctor for small things or calling up relatives to find out about the problems of infancy.

On top of that, you have to do the other household chores which you could easily escape in a joint family system. All this excessive work, running around and tension of bringing up the baby without any help keeps your stress levels very high and you start feeling fatigued very soon.

The Stress Factor

Sheela got separated from her in-laws when her daughter was barely two months old. She tried her best to manage everything but due to the burden of extra work, she became weak and tired. She was also neglecting her health. Her husband was not of much help either as he came back quite late from the office.

One day, as Sheela was out shopping, she felt giddy and fell down unconscious. The baby fell from her arms and started crying. There was a big commotion in the shop. Luckily, one of Sheela's neighbours spotted her and took her home. The baby was badly hurt and needed immediate medical attention. Sheela's husband was on tour. She had no choice but to call her in-laws and seek help.

Stress Buster

Health is wealth. Excess work can be managed by hiring help in the form of maid if you have no one else to turn to. You must keep in mind that you can only look after your home and child if you are fit and healthy. If you feel that you cannot manage alone then it is better to swallow your pride and patch up with your in-laws.

Say No to Stress

Just like this child is the apple of your eyes, similarly, your in-laws also love their grandchild. So do not shy away from them. Even if you are not living with them, maintain congenial relationships. They will extend all the help they can. This will certainly be much better than having to call them in an emergency and being labelled as a careless mother and a selfish daughter-in-law.

Creative Thinking

Parents are always there to help us. They would never disappoint their own children. Give them due respect and get lots of love from them in return.

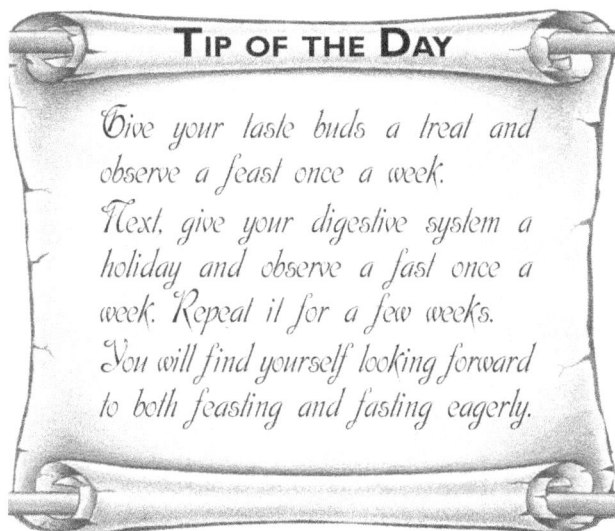

TIP OF THE DAY

Give your taste buds a treat and observe a feast once a week.

Next, give your digestive system a holiday and observe a fast once a week. Repeat it for a few weeks. You will find yourself looking forward to both feasting and fasting eagerly.

Stress with Hubby

One day Akbar was furious with his wife. In a fit of rage, he ordered his wife to leave his palace and go to her father's house. The queen was very upset. She called for Birbal. After narrating the entire episode, she asked for his advice. Birbal pacified her, "Do not worry. Such quarrels do occur in a family. Just do as I tell you and all will be well."

So the next day, the queen asked Emperor Akbar, "Your Majesty, I will do as you wish. But since I will not be seeing you again for the rest of my life, I would like to invite you to my palace for dinner tonight. Also please allow me to take with me my most precious possession that I may keep as your memoir."

The emperor agreed

That night, Akbar went to the queen's palace for dinner. She had prepared all his favourite dishes. At the end of the dinner, she offered him a glass of milk. The queen had added sleeping pills in the milk. As soon as Akbar finished the glass of milk, he fell asleep. The queen sent for Birbal.

Birbal arrived with a carriage. Akbar was put into the carriage and sent with the queen to her father's house. The next morning when Akbar woke up he looked around him puzzled. He felt strange. The room seemed unfamiliar. Then he saw the queen sitting at his bedside. She said, "Pardon me, my Lord. But you are in my father's house. If you remember, yesterday, you had granted me a wish to carry my most precious possession with me. So I have brought you along with me."

Akbar was touched by his wife's love. He realised his own folly and returned to the palace with the queen.

Love can overcome animosity.

Peaceful action against unreasonable opposition achieves the best results.

Silence is the hardest argument which can sometimes be offered to your opponent.

Made for Each Other

> Each person needs to be loved in his or her own special way. The key to it is to understand and to speak that person's language of love

Love is the central element in a successful marriage. If that exists, all problems get sorted out. When you contemplate marriage, in your mind you have accepted that you want to build a relationship. The dreams, hopes and aspirations of two people are involved. When new relationships are formed, adjustments are imminent.

Stress Factor

Sunita is married for ten years now. Her life has been sailing smoothly. She has a loving husband, two children and all material comforts. Yet she feels incomplete. She misses the love and attention showered by her husband in the initial years of marriage. She feels that her husband no longer finds her attractive and that is the reason why, he does not give her enough time. She cribs over it and often suffers from mood swings. Her husband tried to make her see reason but when nothing worked, he too gave up.

Stress Buster

You expect the same treatment from your hubby as you received in the initial years of marriage but have you ever thought of giving him the similar treatment too? He is not complaining then why are you? As time passes, responsibilities increase and your time is divided. You still love each other but demonstrating this love takes a back seat. So do not feel stressed. Your husband is a sincere person. Your love is not lost, it has only matured over the years.

Say No to Stress

Cribbing or sitting in a corner and brooding for hours is not the best way to get your husband's attention. Put on your best clothes and cheerfully welcome him as he comes back home. Give him a surprise treat once in a while and revel in the glow that lights up in his eyes. Going for a stroll after dinner is a good idea. It boosts your health as well as the emotional equation. Plan a trip or an outing together. Leave the kids in the care of your parents or in-laws. You will come back refreshed.

Creative Thinking

You were made for each other and that is why you are together. Do not let small events of life make you feel let down. Love is hiding behind the doors. Just knock and doors will open up for you.

TIP OF THE DAY

Treat yourself to saunas and steam treatments. Sweat out toxins through steam and sauna. If you can do it together in the close proximity of your home, nothing like it.

Sharing the Burden

Most housewives depend upon their husbands for everything starting from financial support to doing teeny-weeny household chores. But this dependence acts like a handicap for them. They lean too much on their husbands. And at any point of time, the husband is not able to do the work, the dependent wife feels stressed.

Stress Factor

Suchitra lived a very cushioned life. As she would never venture out of the house for shopping or other outside chores, her husband took over the responsibility. Even shopping for groceries, buying vegetables were all done by her husband on his way home. Suchitra only looked after the home. One fine day, her husband came home and informed her about his promotion and two months of training in Nagpur. She was devastated. How will she manage without him for two months? The thought of spending two months alone without anyone for support was a dreadful thought. The thought haunted her so much that she went into depression. Her husband tried to make her see the advantages of his training but the stress she was facing was beyond her control. Finally, her husband had to forego the promotion and cancel his training in Nagpur.

Stress Busters

Is your dependence upon your husband costing him dear? Don't you think it is better to learn to be independent? In any case, being independent gives you a confidence. This confidence shows in your personality. All the housewives are well educated today. So why depend upon your husband for doing outside work? You can very well share his responsibilities. Be a helping hand, not a burden.

Say No to Stress

What makes you more stressed? A harassed, tired and short the tempered husband who does the outside work because you are unable to do it; or going out of the house and doing the jobs yourself. Choose your options carefully and see what benefits you more. Naturally, the latter is good for you as well as your hubby. At least, he won't snap at you now over trivial matters.

Creative Thinking

Earn your confidence by being independent. Your husband will love you for the new glow on your face.

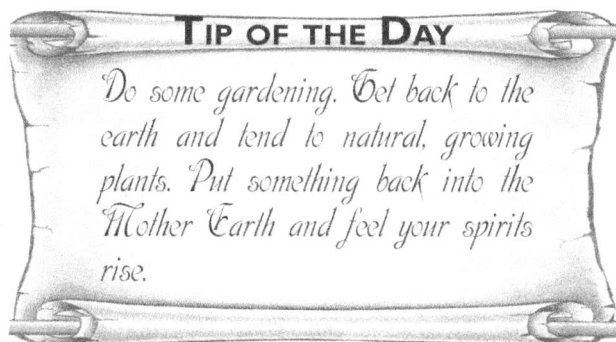

TIP OF THE DAY

Do some gardening. Get back to the earth and tend to natural, growing plants. Put something back into the Mother Earth and feel your spirits rise.

Budget Makers

Give your wife a Diamond necklace and she will always say, that she wanted an Emerald one.

Since a housewife is not working, so naturally, she has no means of regular earning. Mostly the husband provides the money for household expenses. That is why, he is called the breadwinner of the house. But whatever amount the husband provides should be utilized wisely. You should be aware of your financial position and should be able to save for a rainy day.

Stress Factor

Harish was the sole breadwinner of the family. His wife Suruchi never bothered to find out about his financial position. He too never indulged her into these matters. One day, as Harish was going to office, his car was crushed under a speeding truck. Harish survived but due to a spinal injury, he went into coma. He had to be operated soon. The operation required about three lakhs which had to be deposited as soon as possible. Suruchi was in a fix. She had no idea about their financial status. She did not even know where Harish kept his money, in which banks he had his accounts or from where she could borrow the money? Her husband was unconscious, so naturally, he was of no help in such a situation. She contacted her relatives and literally begged for help. When nothing came out, she sold her jewellery, mortgaged the house and deposited the required amount. After Harish recovered and came back home, he asked his wife as to how she managed to pay the money. He was aghast on being told that she had to mortgage the house for money. He took out the bank passbook and some bank FD's from his briefcase and showed her. Together they all contained more than five lakhs rupees. If only Suruchi knew about their financial position, she could have easily used that money instead of mortgaging the house. Now they had to pay a much bigger price to get their house back.

Stress Buster

This is only one situation, we have taken up. There are many more everyday incidents, which point towards the fact, that money matters should be discussed among the husband and wife even if the wife is not working.

Dependence upon your husband can bring your stress levels high. Financial independence does not mean having to go out of the house to work. You can learn these things even by being a housewife. Learn about your finances. Go to the bank to deposit your cheques or withdraw the money. In this way, you will help yourself by being updated on your financial status.

Say No to Stress

If you have a keen interest in money, you may take tips from your husband and start investing in shares. Preparing a family budget together will also give you an insight on how to spend wisely. It will also help you get your priorities right.

Creative Thinking

Demonstrating your dependence on your husband in financial matters will only make you vulnerable and open to criticism. Money is important in life. So learn how to deal with it in a proper way.

TIP OF THE DAY

Do not live your life for other people all the time. Take out some time to try something that might not necessarily please everyone else but would give you great pleasure. Better to have had your wish than wish you had.

Taking Each Other for Granted

> Real pleasure is in giving and not in receiving.

Each one of us has a goal in life – to be happy. I sincerely believe that you should get happiness out of small things in life or you will never know what happiness is. Giving due respect to each other and to your relationship will give you a deep sense of happiness whereas taking each other for granted will not only make life monotonous but it will also rob you of all the joys and pleasures of exploring new horizons.

Stress Factor

Ranjan and Manju are married for six years now. Manju is a housewife and would sit the whole day in the house waiting for Ranjan to come back. Initially, Ranjan used to come back on time. Manju would then give all the details of her day's activities which Ranjan would listen amidst the sips of hot tea. But for sometime now, Ranjan has made it a habit to come home late, have dinner and go to sleep. Manju keeps waiting for him all evening. But he does not talk to her much. He takes Manju for granted. He knows she is there to cook, to look after his home and children. She feels as if he is treating her as a part of the furniture in the house which has been brought in and used to its maximum advantage. He does not talk to her or lend her a responsive ear either. Manju hates Ranjan's attitude but cannot help it. All that she can do is cry her heart out at night only to wake up to live another day with the same monotonous routine.

Stress Buster

Look within yourself before you point a finger at your husband. He was not like this earlier. He gave you time and attention earlier but then you started taking him for granted. You would blabber off all your problems the moment he entered the house without even thinking that the poor tired soul might need some rest first. Grow up and learn to solve your own problems instead of telling your husband about the silly little difficulties of the day. Make it a rule not to tell your husband anything unpleasant till he has his tea and settled down. The heavens won't fall! If nothing happened the entire day, another half an hour will not make much of a difference. Your husband wants some peace of mind when he comes home.

Say No to Stress

Do not nag, do not shout, do not pester. Do not take your relationship with your better half for granted. Do not throw tantrums. Let your husband relax after a day's hard work and enjoy those quiet moments together. Discuss your problems with him when he is in a better frame of mind. Give new dimensions to your relationship and it will fill your life with new happiness.

Creative Thinking

Think of all the good times both of you have spent together. Try to rekindle the same magic. Use soft music, soft lighting and good food to enhance his mood. Believe me, by the time, he is ready to listen to your problems, you too would be so relaxed that you will find it inappropriate to mention them at this magic hour.

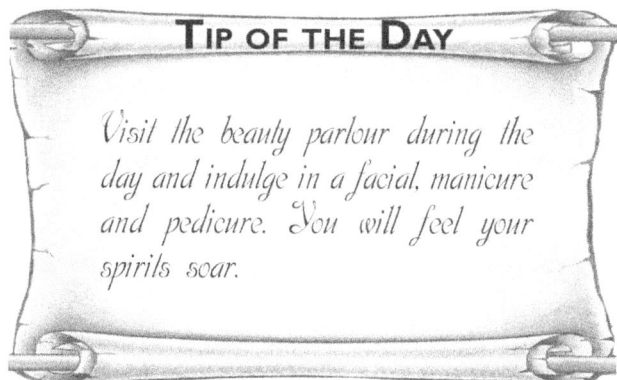

TIP OF THE DAY

Visit the beauty parlour during the day and indulge in a facial, manicure and pedicure. You will feel your spirits soar.

At Your Mercy

> A good memory is one that can remember a day's blessings and forget the day's troubles.

Dependence on your husband can certainly bring your stress levels to soar. You cannot control the other person. If you depend on him to a great extent then there are chances that he may not come up to your expectations each time. And every time, you find a job unsatisfactory, you will get tensed because first of all the work is pending and secondly, you feel cheated as your expectations were high due to your dependence on him for all matters.

Stress Factor

Ranjita would depend upon her husband for fixing things in the house, for taking her shopping, to deposit bills and many other sundry jobs. She would give the excuse that she did not know how to drive, so how could she move around? One day, when her husband was on tour, the kitchen faucet started leaking. She tried to put some cloth on it to stop the flow but nothing seemed to work. The more she tried, the worse it became. She called the plumber but he was out on call. The flow of water was so much that it had started seeping into the dining room threatening the precious rug. Ranjita was in a fix when suddenly, the door bell rang. It was her neighbour, Sudha. Seeing her worried expression, Sudha enquired about the problem. When Ranjita told her, Sudha asked her to show the tap which was leaking. On seeing the tap, Sudha simply bent down and turned off the main supply to the faucet. In no time, the flow of water stopped and Ranjita heaved a sigh of relief. The two friends had a hearty laugh, but in her heart, Ranjita felt embarrassed for being so ignorant. If only she had taken some interest in things which she always thought to be a male-dominated territory then she would not have faced such a problem.

Stress Buster

All the housewives are well educated today. So why depend upon your husband for doing menial work. With a little effort on your part you can very well handle jobs such as getting small things fixed around the house, deposit electricity and telephone bills and do the weekly shopping for groceries. If you have a car, learn to drive. This will make you mobile and you will fell independent. Being on your own will help you complete the jobs on time and save you a lot of unnecessary tension.

Say No to Stress

Why should you be at someone's mercy? Women are no less than men. There is no more division of territories now. If men can be the best cooks, why can't you be a plumber or an electrician for a change?

Creative Thinking

It is better to be independent so that you can organise your jobs according to their priorities and do them on time. Independence will bring new happiness in your life. You will feel more confident and self assured. And your hubby will admire you and welcome your new found status.

TIP OF THE DAY

There is bound to be a good way to get you in a good mood - you just have to find it.

- Fix a mega sandwich.
- Take a bath with essential oils.
- Take a brisk walk.
- Call a friend for a chat or
- Repair something in the house.

You are My Confidante

> A sound relationship is not based on complete frankness, it is based on tact.

You could do well to remember that with your hubby, as in all human relationships, too much honesty can create problems. All delicately balanced relationships require us to blunt the sharp cutting edge of truth with diplomacy and tact.

Stress Factor

When Shuchi was in college, she fell in love with a muslim boy. Since her parents were totally against the match, she sacrificed her love and agreed to marry the boy of her parent's choice. Anil was a handsome young man who was very loving. Shuchi was besotted by his charms. They got along well too. They got married amidst much fanfare and soon after, they headed to Shimla for their honeymoon.

During some intimate and emotional moments, Shuchi admitted to Anil, about her affair with a muslim boy. While coaxing her in telling him all her love affairs before marriage, Anil had promised not to take it to heart.

But once the truth was out, he could not digest the fact that his wife was in love with someone else before marriage. Their ten-day long honeymoon was shrunk to two days and they were back home, the third day itself.

Shuchi began her married life on shaky grounds just because she forgot to blunt the sharp edge of truth.

Stress Buster

Your husband may be your best friend, still there are a few things which are best unsaid. Put yourself in your husband's place and imagine your own reaction to such outbursts. Since our childhood, we have been taught to be honest and never to tell a lie. But a lie is not a lie if it is told for something good. So understand the temperament and psychology of your husband and act accordingly. Do not just blabber whatever comes to your mind. Be tactful and let peace prevail.

Say No to Stress

In your life, you will be faced with many such situations where you will have to think twice before uttering the truth. In such cases, it is better to be tactful than to spoil your relations by telling the truth. Your husband may be very caring, understanding and a true angel still there may be a weak spot in his heart, which you may hurt by being blunt about a touching subject.

Creative Thinking

Ignorance is bliss. What you do not know does not hurt you.

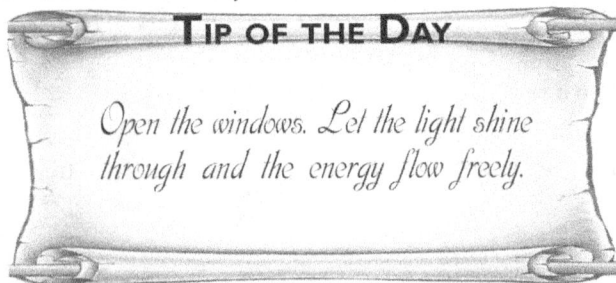

TIP OF THE DAY

Open the windows. Let the light shine through and the energy flow freely.

Pati Parmeshwar

> It is your judgement that keep you from joy and expectations which make you unhappy

God made men and women equal. Over the years, our system adopted the fact that man is superior to woman, primarily because a man is physically stronger than a woman. But when you marry, you marry for love. And two people are always at par in love.

Stress Factor

Sugandha was a well educated girl with modern views. She got married in a rich but orthodox family. Her in-laws lived in Bikaner. They had a family business which was jointly run by her father-in-law and her husband who was their only son. Everything was fine till that fateful day when Sugandha discovered that her husband was addicted to vices like drinking, gambling and also visited brothels. She was shocked and raised a hue and cry in the house.

She thought, her husband who was so affectionate till now will understand and promise to amend his ways. But her mother-in-law came to her son's rescue and started preaching Sugandha on the significance of *Pati Parmeshwar*.

First, she tried to pacify Sugandha, when she refused to give in, she got angry and told Sugandha to shut up in clear terms. She said, "Your *Pati* is your God. How dare you raise your voice against him?" Sugandha was stunned. If she were wrong, would her husband have forgiven her so easily?

Stress Buster

Your husband is a human being just like you. Why accord him the status of God if he does not deserve it? You are two individuals married to each other with a number of vices and virtues. Why not accept each other as human beings and try to amend the faults in each other? However, turning a blind eye to all your husband's faults just because he is your *Pati Parmeshwar* is not correct.

Say No to Stress

Gone are the days when a husband was considered to be God by his wife. Today, both are on equal footing. So giving the status of God to the husband is neither advisable nor practical. He is as much a human being as you are, so why give this special treatment to him and create unnecessary stress in the house?

Creative Thinking

Your husband is your partner for life. He comes from the same mould in which you are made. Love him, adore him, fight with him, care for him, but do not worship him. That puts him on a pedestal so high up that you may not be able to relate to him normally.

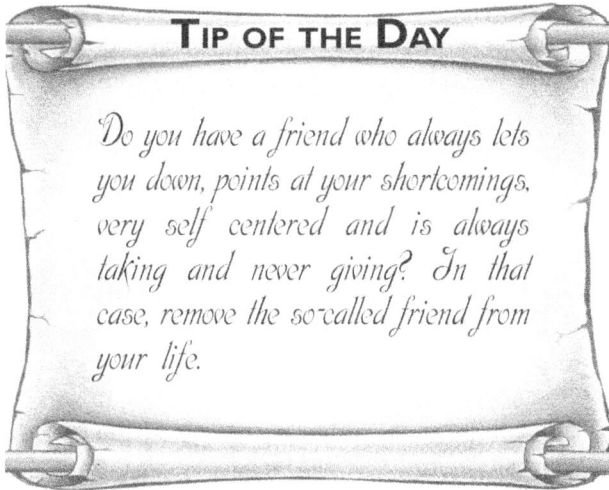

TIP OF THE DAY

Do you have a friend who always lets you down, points at your shortcomings, very self centered and is always taking and never giving? In that case, remove the so-called friend from your life.

Extramarital Affairs

> Infidelity is not committed on an impulse,
> but by a series of small things brought together.

Marriage is a commitment for life. Infidelity in marriage is not acceptable. There are many causes for indulging into extramarital affairs. There may be conflicts between the spouses. There may be heated exchanges which turn hostile. Then there may be a communication gap. Silence, at times, harbours internal seething which may erupt anytime. Then there are sexual adjustments which form the very basis of a marriage. Maladjustments in this area pose marital risk. Spouses may turn rebellious giving way to extra marital relationships. The biggest problem is the personal attitude of one or both the partners. People fail to understand their own feelings. They fail to appreciate the love in their lives. They fail to understand that marriage is a lifelong relationship where the couple should be committed to each other.

Stress Factor

Rishita's husband was having an affair with his secretary. When Rishita came to know about it, she was aghast. She could not believe her ears. But when she saw the two of them coming out of a hotel room like a lovey-dovey couple, there was no room left for doubt. Her world was shattered. She had two small children to look after and she was not earning either. She was totally dependent on her husband for everything. What would she do? If she encounters him, he may decide to leave her for that woman. And if she kept quite, her conscience pricked her. The stress was killing her.

Stress Buster

In such a situation, children are your biggest assets. Every father loves his children and feels responsible towards them. He would definitely not want to deprive them of his love and affection. Do not involve the children in the matter, but rest assured that half your battle is won. Now look at the other things. Delve on the areas which could have led him to go astray. Is it your behaviour towards him, is your appearance not very appealing, have you put on too much weight, have you lost him because you could not keep the magic alive in your marriage? etc. Find out the reason behind his going to the other woman, and try to rectify it.

Say No to Stress

Extramarital affairs can certainly take their toll on you. It is like a jolt to your ego. It shakes you up completely. The person whom you always thought belonged to you, is now shared by someone else too. This stress is enough to take you into the deep valleys of depression. But crying or feeling stressed is not the solution to this problem. Look for the areas in which you lack, and which could have led your man to go astray. If you rectify your faults then there are less chances of your man going away from you.

Consider a situation, in which a husband comes home from a day's hard work. He feels like relaxing over a cup of tea with a refreshing chat with his wife. But what he gets in return is a frown on her face, a list of complaints and a much delayed tea. Instead of sharing the day's events, his wife gives a long list of troubles created by the children during the day. The final straw comes when she hands him over the shopping list. To escape her fury, the poor man goes to the market much against his wishes to buy the grocery. All this is unnecessary stress which could have been avoided. Such situations may lead to the man staying away from home for longer hours and may end up with an extramarital affair.

Creative Thinking

It's never too late to try. He has loved you, and he still loves you. It's only lust that has taken over for the time being. He will definitely come back to you with some efforts on your part.

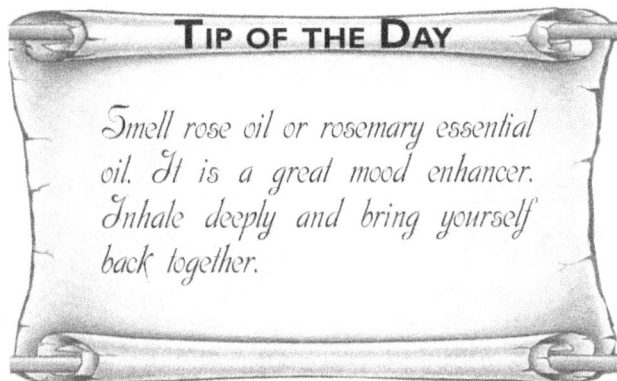

TIP OF THE DAY

Smell rose oil or rosemary essential oil. It is a great mood enhancer. Inhale deeply and bring yourself back together.

Stress with Children

Akbar once saw a woman hugging and kissing a child that did not look particularly appealing. Akbar expressed surprise that a woman could lavish so much love on such an unattractive child.

"That's because it's her own child", explained Birbal, "to a mother her child is the most beautiful in the world."

"How can that be", the emperor was not satisfied by Birbal's explanation.

The next day, Birbal called a guard and in the presence of Emperor Akbar ordered him to bring the most beautiful child to the palace.

The following day, the guard came to the palace with a small boy with buck teeth and hair that stood up like porcupine quills and hesitantly pushed him in front of Akbar.

"The most beautiful child, Your Majesty." He said in a hesitant voice.

"How do you know he is beautiful?" asked Akbar.

"My wife, his mother, says so." Replied the guard.

There is no arguing with a mother's love. It is consistent and unshakeable. Nothing can suppress it. If we can be half as consistent in our relationships and in our dealings with our dear ones, half our problems will be solved.

Kiddies Corner

> Your child is like a book which you cannot
> read when it is too close or too distant

C hildren spell responsibility and no responsibility is free of stress and worry. Bringing up children is a matter of joy with some traces of stress and worries.

This is perhaps the best phase in a housewife's life. In many cases, motherhood is the deciding factor for a woman choosing to be a housewife. This is the beginning of a new life for the mother and the child, both. When the baby is small, the mother keeps worrying about his growth, eating pattern, etc. She spends sleepless nights to meet the demands of the infant. Cooperation from the family members boosts her morale and she does not feel fatigued or stressed. But if she does not get any support from her husband or in-laws, then the situation becomes very tiring for her. The joy of motherhood turns into stressful moments of despair.

Stress Factor

Nita got married to the younger son of the Malhotra household. Her elder sister-in-law had a two-year old son. A year later, Nita also gave birth to a baby boy. Celebrations filled the house with joy and laughter. Everyone was happy. As time passed, Nita's son started growing and started crossing each milestone of childhood. Nita felt happy to see her baby growing. But there was a problem, each time her baby would miss a milestone even by a month, her mother-in-law would start comparing him with the elder sister-in-law's son. "Aditya started smiling when he was just two weeks old, why hasn't Abhishek started smiling till now?

He is almost a month old now", or Aditya cut his first tooth in the fifth month, but Abhishek is in his seventh month now, still no signs of cutting teeth, etc." The comparison irked Nita very much. Although, each time she consulted the pediatrician about Abhishek's progress, he would give a satisfying nod. Still a doubt lurched in her mind because of the comparisons made by her mother-in-law. She felt as if her son was a laggard and it made her restless and tense.

Stress Busters

"My child started walking when she was nine months old" or "she spoke her first words before she cut her first tooth" and so on. The list is endless. Every mother takes pride in her children's achievements. There are milestones set by doctors for the baby's growth taking an average child in consideration. So if your child did not manage to achieve some of these milestones, don't fret. Getting agitated over such trivial matters will be of no use. Remember, all children are not alike. Some are fast learners, while some are slow learners. But sooner or later, they all come round and grow up into normal, healthy children.

Say No to Stress

The role of parents is a unique one. Do not compare your children's growth with others. And if others do so then do not feel bad about it. You cannot stop anyone from voicing their opinion. Have faith in your child, God and your genes. You will sail through.

Creative Thinking

After you are through with this phase and you look back in retrospect, then you will find yourself smiling at your own foolishness. The stress which you experienced at that time was of no consequence – this you will realise later.

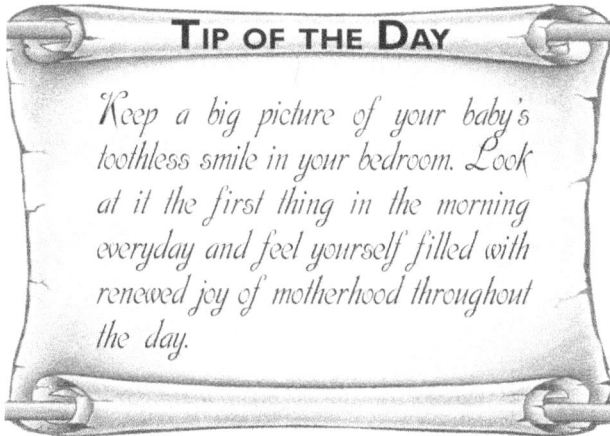

TIP OF THE DAY

Keep a big picture of your baby's toothless smile in your bedroom. Look at it the first thing in the morning everyday and feel yourself filled with renewed joy of motherhood throughout the day.

High Expectations

Small children depend on their mothers for each and every thing. It is a delight for them to have their mother around them. That is why a homemaker plays a very important role in shaping the future of her children. But remember one thing, never expect anything from anybody. This includes your children too. Children are like delicate, innocent buds which are yet to bloom. Expecting them to show results before time is asking too much from them.

Stress Factor

Ria was Sudha's only child. She was quite intelligent. Sudha had high expectations from her. When Ria was young, Sudha enrolled her in various hobby classes so that she could become an all rounder. Ria would go for swimming, painting, dance and music classes regularly besides attending normal school. During summer vacation, her routine would be very tight, what with more hobby courses like computer, creative writing, western dance and music, clay modelling, etc., keeping the little girl busy throughout the day. Ria would have loved to play 'ghar-ghar' with her friends, but Sudha forced her to play games like—chess, monopoly and scrabble. During Ria's Xth board exams, Sudha was continuously hovering around her coaxing her to study. The results were far from satisfying. Sudha was devastated. As she was about to reprimand her daughter on such low grades, she was met with a gory sight on entering Ria's bedroom. Ria had committed suicide by hanging herself to the ceiling.

Sudha's world came crashing down. What had she gained by putting so much pressure on her poor child all these years? A good life was wasted due to the stress and tensions which were pressed on to the child through the mother.

Stress Busters

Never keep your expectations too high. Treat your child as an average child. Reward them with your biggest hug if they achieve something, but do not punish them for not achieving something. We see many cases around us where either parents or children themselves went into depression for not having achieved the desired targets. Please don't play in the hands of fate. Keep your cool and let life take its own course. Remember, 'all's well that ends well.'

Say No to Stress

Children are your assets, don't turn them into your liabilities. Give them time and space to spread their wings. Life of a housewife is full of stress. Starting from the birth of her child to the day the child grows up into an adult, the housewife experiences stress in different forms. But living with stress for such a long time is not good. So it's better for her to manage her stress levels by taking a positive and relaxed view of life instead of passing it on to her children.

Creative Thinking

They are your children not slaves. You brought them into this world but you did not give them life. So why try to control it?

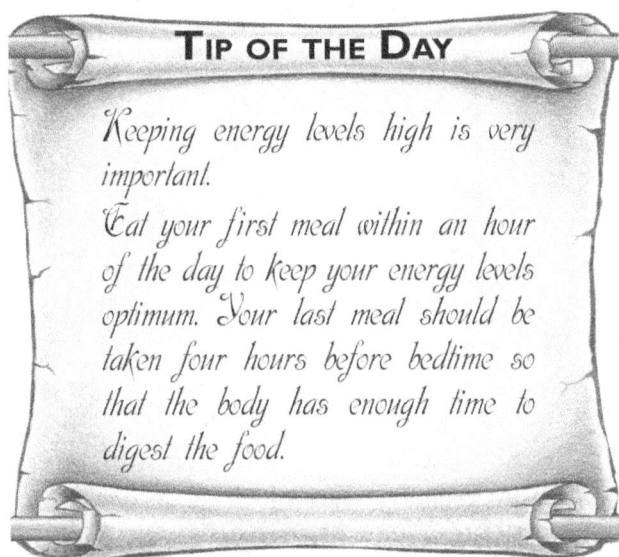

TIP OF THE DAY

Keeping energy levels high is very important.

Eat your first meal within an hour of the day to keep your energy levels optimum. Your last meal should be taken four hours before bedtime so that the body has enough time to digest the food.

Am I a Servant?

> There is no friendship and
> no love like that of a parent

The love, care and protection that a housewife provides in the growing years of her children can never be substituted by a maid, grandparents or a creche as in the case of a working woman. But once children grow up, they start weaving their own world. They get too engrossed within their own group of friends, studies and outings. Unwittingly, they start distancing themselves from the mother. As they grow, they start detesting the caring attitude of their mother and take it as an interference in their independent way of living. In such a case, the poor mother, who has spent many years tending her kids feels at a loss and does not know where she went wrong. All of a sudden, stress crops within her. She feels hurt and dejected but does not find an escape route for her emotions.

Stress Factor

Sunita was a village girl. She married Satish who was an electrician in Patna. In a few years, she became the mother of a son and a daughter. In the meantime, Satish got a good job in Mumbai and the family shifted there. They lived in a chawl. It was a new experience for Sunita. Satish admitted the children in good schools. Time passed by. Satish's work expanded and the family shifted to their own small house in the suburbs. The children were in college now. They spoke fluent English and wore trendy clothes. But there was a major change in their behaviour. They would treat their mother very badly. Sunita could neither speak nor understand English.

Her children started treating her as a servant. They would shout at her slightest mistake and make fun of her in English which she could not understand. Although Satish was also not very educated, still the children feared him because he was the provider of the family. Sunita would cry her heart out when alone, but she loved her children dearly so she never said anything to them. But the tension of being treated badly was taking its toll on her health.

Stress Buster

The worst part of her dilemma arrived when she was needed only for the housework in the house. Apart from that, her adolescent children treated her badly. In her mind, this kind of behaviour automatically transformed her from a housewife and a mother to a mere servant.

And the worst part was that she couldn't share this pain and feeling of hurt with anyone because it had been inflicted upon her by her own loved ones.

Say No to Stress

Getting your husband into confidence is a good idea. Being the stronger of the two parents, he can easily make the children see sense and correct their wrong behaviour. Remember living with stress for a long time is not good. So it's better for you to manage your stress levels soon by taking a positive and relaxed view of life.

Creative Thinking

Be strong. They are your children. You have brought them up. Why should you take all this rubbish from them? Be a no nonsense mother and show them who is the boss around here.

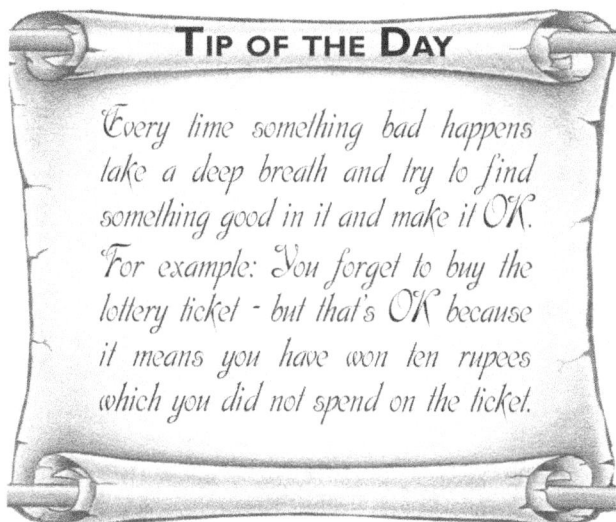

TIP OF THE DAY

Every time something bad happens take a deep breath and try to find something good in it and make it OK. For example: You forget to buy the lottery ticket - but that's OK because it means you have won ten rupees which you did not spend on the ticket.

Handling Adolescents

> Praise your children openly,
> reprove them secretly

As children grow, it becomes difficult to handle them. As adolescents, they turn into a bunch of rebels who need to be tamed tactfully from time to time. Adolescence is a very crucial juncture for children. They should be handled properly otherwise they may turn astray.

Stress Factor

My cousin, Rima has two teenaged daughters. They were very loving, affectionate and obedient till they were in school. Once I went to her house. Her daughters had joined college by then. As I sat enquiring about her daughters, one of them entered the room. Apparently, she was going to college. What surprised me most were her clothes and the manner in which she carried herself. She was wearing a skimpy top and skin tight trousers. She wished me by nodding and spoke to her mother in a very gruff voice. Gone was the plain, simple, homely sweet girl, I had seen the last time. She had come to borrow some money. In a jiffy, she was out of the house. Before I could ask anything from my cousin, she broke down. She told me how her daughter had changed since she joined college. While she was blaming the college and her friends for everything, I kept on thinking about the other girls who go to college and still retain their values and traditions. The girl was obviously not guided properly by the parents. It was later revealed by the mother, that she had been very strict with her daughters from the very beginning for the fear that they do not fall in bad company. She had put them in a girl's school, never allowed them to interact with boys and always kept their reins tightly in her hands. Till the daughters were in school, there was not much exposure, and they remained within limits. But college opened new horizons for them and now they felt free to fly as they wished. They stopped bowing to the strict rules laid by their mother. 'What would happen to her daughters?' — This thought would nag Rima day and night and she felt miserable.

Stress Buster

When you get stressed over your adolescent's behaviour, it is easier to blame squarely on the children. But we, as parents, too have a part to play. On our part, we should also allow youngsters some breathing space. Be an emotional anchor to them whenever they need it. Help them choose a satisfying career and stand by their decision. It is a rapidly changing world. You should give them little time to adapt, to make their choices, to follow their dreams. It's true that children are not always correct, nor are you. So learn to accept your mistakes in front of them. This will teach them modesty and they will also willingly admit their own mistakes. After making all these efforts, you are most likely to share a congenial relationship. Hence, the stress is managed automatically and in the most efficient manner.

Say No to Stress

Once in a while, all children bring their friends home. So when adolescent children bring their friends home, why should you feel perturbed? College life is much diverse. Children from all over the country come and study together. Naturally, they have different styles, moves and philosophies. Feeling stressed over this matter will not be of any use. You should have confidence in your own child.

Creative Thinking

Children are your heart and soul. They should be nurtured with love and care. Instead of eyeing all their actions suspiciously, have faith in them. Keep watch on them from a distance, do not interfere unnecessarily. Intervene when required, preach when asked for, guide when they are faltering — this is the key to good parenting.

TIP OF THE DAY

If something bad happens, think of four steps to turn it into something good.
Suppose Your maid did not come today! Here are the four steps to make you feel good.

- Doing housework will give you the required exercise.
- You can take your afternoon nap peacefully without having to wait for her arrival.
- You can clean all the cobwebs today which you have been putting off.
- You are your own master, you can do the work as and when you feel like.

The Pawns

> If we do what is necessary,
> all the odds will be in our favour

C hildren can be your best companions. They can be your source of joy. They can be your pride. But never turn them into your pawns. Life is not a game of chess. You cannot always make calculated moves. If you try to do so then life loses its charm and you lose the love and respect of others.

The Stress Factor

Athira was blessed with a son and daughter. The son was about eight years old and the daughter was two years old. Athira never had a good relationship with her in-laws. Though they lived in the same house, Athira lived on the first floor and her in-laws stayed on the ground floor. Athira was always suspicious of her in-laws. She would keep on spying on them, as to what they were doing, where were they going, what were they giving to their daughter and so on. Earlier, she used to ask all these things from her husband. When he got tired of answering these questions, she started asking the maidservant who also worked for her in-laws. The maid was a big gossipmonger. She would exaggerate things and tell Athira in a spicy manner. Somehow her mother-in-law got the wind of this. So she removed the maid. Now Athira had no other way of finding out as to what her in-laws are up to. This time, she thought of a new pawn in the form of her own son. She would coax her son to spend more time with the grandparents and when he came back home, she would ask him each and every detail. As the son grew up, he understood the subtle ways of his mother. He was genuinely fond of his grandparents. So he started spending more time with them. Now Athira was all the more worried. She felt that her in-laws had taken her son away from her. Her husband who was a silent spectator till now, opened his mouth and lashed his wife rudely for her wrong behaviour. Athira was aghast. It was the maze of her own creation from which she could not find an escape route.

Stress Busters

Some daughter-in-laws make the mistake of turning their children into pawns in their ongoing battles with their in-laws. This is wrong for it is not only foolish on your part, but it can also be harmful for the children. Children can serve as an ideal bridge between you and your in-laws because you both love them equally. Children may even help to keep channels of communication open during a cold war but using them as pawns to get information about their activities is a strict, 'no'. Instead, encourage your children to be close to their grandparents in good faith. There is a lot they can learn from their grandparents, which they will not find in text books or which you may not be able to teach them for want of time and patience. Values such as caring, sharing and giving are best taught by the grandparents for they have at their command a wealth of wisdom distilled from experience.

Say No to Stress

Remember, your in-laws are not your enemies. They are not out to snatch your children away. If your children love their grandparents, it does not mean they love you any less. So stop glaring at your in-laws, when they hug your children or buy special gifts for them. They are not out to bribe the children and steal their affection. They are merely conveying their affection towards them.

Creative Thinking

Grandparents can be a big support when it comes to raising your children. In today's hectic life, who has the time to sit with the children playing umpteen games, or telling them fairy tales or listening to the events of their day at school or feeding them patiently, spoon after spoon with love and affection. Only a grandparent can give such care.

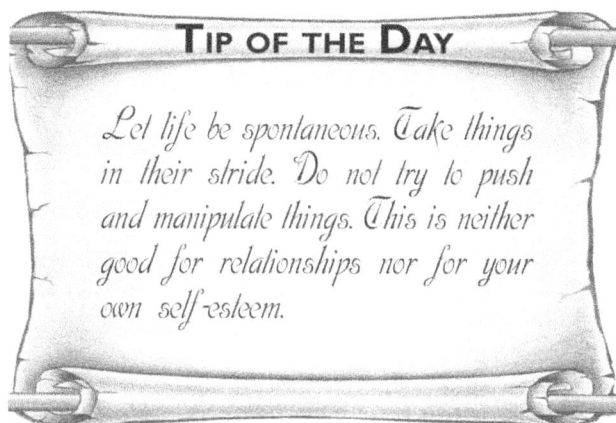

TIP OF THE DAY

Let life be spontaneous. Take things in their stride. Do not try to push and manipulate things. This is neither good for relationships nor for your own self-esteem.

Also Available
in Hindi

Also Available
in Hindi

Also Available
in Kannada, Tamil

Also Available
in Kannada

Also Available
in Kannada

STRESS MANAGEMENT